TEARS OF THE WOUNDED
MY ONLY WORDS
LIFE
DEATH
SPOKEN TRUTH
VOL 2

Tears of the Wounded
#SpokenTruth

Table of Contents

This book is a work of fictitious names - the characters, places, and incidents are either products of the author's imagination or are used fictitiously. Any resemblance to actual persons (living or dead), events, or locations is entirely coincidental.

The reproduction or utilization of this work in whole or part in any form, whether electronic, digital, mechanical or by other means, now known or hear after invented, including xerography, photocopying, scanning, recording, or any information storage or retrieval system is forbidden without prior written permission of the author.

<u>ACKNOWLEDGMENTS</u>

I would love to thank every person I know individually, but I know that is impossible. Thankfully, I can leave messages in every book I sign. Here are a few that, without their support, trust, kind words, constructive criticism and faith…you would not know me to be the person I am today. In no particular order (if you do not see your name and you are close to me) you should never question how much you mean to me.

My sister, Ms. Crawford; Wilysha, Bola, Nneoma, Tiffany J, Bro. Washington, Julian, Randy, Kay Renee, Dee, Opal, Shawonna Wynn, DJ Knots, Tracy Haynes, Joe, Alyx, Jean, Prophet, Mena, Bree, Della Della, Frank, Adam, Celia, CiearaCiara, Lil D, Yung Chuck, Candice Coffie, Siaara Freeman, L. J. Hamilton, Natasha, Monique, Floww, Dave, Monika, Drew, Spyda, Shanez, Fallon, Shawna D, Dontay, Ruth, Paula, Hunter, Sylvia, HennaC, MacNova, Omega, Mag, JoyaVeli, T-Diamond, Microphone Rome. To every soul in my city, from the day laborers to the tenure teachers, from the trap house keepers to the police on the beat, from the Anarchist to the highest elected office---to every person I've ever worked with (even if it was just for the day). For all the organizers and protesters that stood side by side with me to make the world a better place. To every person I've ever shared a stage or mic with. Thank you!! Thank ALL of you!!!

And for all of those who said I wouldn't make it, who told me to give up and get a job…I'm hiring. Finally, to my Manager, Debra Sue: Thank you for seeing what I could not see and for believing in me.

INTRODUCTIONS

Thank you so much for grabbing a volume from me. This book is me… my flaws, hopes, dreams, failures, and truth. This book contains poetry, short stories, illustrations, and truth as only I could write and draw it. It has not been an easy journey from the first book to this one, but you have a copy, so I must be doing something right.

When you see #SpokenTruth throughout the book, those are verses that I memorized and performed all over the country by the time of this publication.

There are seven chapters, illustrations, quotes, and first draft dates; each one representing a different path of my life. When you finish, I hope you will have a better view of who I once was and how much LIFE means to me.

Much love; thank you with all my heart.

<u>PREFACE</u>

So, right now I have a lot of things going on. Unfortunately, it comes at a time when I am financially restructuring, trying to figure out and juggle between being an entertainer, active activist, author, cook, promoter, computer analyst, builder, poet, inspirational speaker, actor and people bridge...all the while not trying to put a value or a dollar amount on what I do. It has been fun, but now I do have to find a minimum to get by. To make a living, and not add something that puts greater financial responsibility on myself.

So, besides the poetry, the books, and the things that you can learn by Googling me...here are some undeniable truths about my life. Ready? This should be interesting:

1. When I was born, I was given one week to live. I had several barbiturates and narcotics in my system; I was premature and would not eat. My mother came in every day until I gained enough weight to where I could be taken from the hospital.

2. Throughout my childhood I always had trouble connecting to people. I preferred the company of books, computers, and nature over people.

3. I was heavyset, wore glasses, and spoke 'proper English' in the hood. My mother, my sister, and I always bounced around from place to place, living no one place for more than 2 years max.

4. After years of drug abuse and doing what she felt she needed to survive on from low income and men who were not there for more than just one night my sister and I were eventually taken by the childcare system.

5. After 4 years, a few foster parents, and my sister being adopted numerous other things which I wish not to tell but only in a book), we were free.

(Continued)

(Continued)

6. One year after my emancipation, our mother was murdered by a serial killer.

7. In my late teens/early twenties, I worked as a day laborer. If you do not know what day labor is, it's a job where every single day your job assignment is different. One day you could be working in the sewer system, the next day you could be repairing roofs and everything in between.

8. During that time I had a child, and that's all you get to know about that.

9. After that I worked in the restaurant field. I prepared food, cooked food, stocked, learned the business aspect of running a restaurant, and did a great deal of promotions for a successful business entity.

10. In my late twenties to present, I have worked at radio stations, night clubs and promotions. In every field and aspect from hosting, working the door, serving drinks, making food, writing my own shows, co-hosting with other very talented people, security, promotion, remodeling, and doing interviews.

11. Now, I do public speaking, activism, write books, perform poetry, give advice to grassroots organizations, and I lead several grassroots organizations. I've done all of this without a car, a degree, handouts, large amounts of money, or even a stable system or place to rest my head.

Stay positive... you are still breathing; you can make it better; don't give up!

SPOKEN
TRUTH

Chapter 1

> Dreams are what make reality worth living, but at some point, you have to wake up to turn your dreams into reality or someone else will. Never believe your dreams are too big or extravagant because only you can put in the hard work to turn them into reality… – J. Summers

…WHO AM I?

SIMPLE MAN #SPOKENTRUTH

November 17, 2014

I would love to live up to the person people make me out to be. Strong-willed, outspoken, never sheds a tear, always has something positive or inspiring to say and always a smile, yes, a smile on my face.

But I am still just a SIMPLE MAN you see, who most of the time is filled with responsibility and regrets; but I hope that this SIMPLE MAN can bring some type of unity into his community while I bear the full weight that I cannot fail because there is no one to catch me if I fall.

Just a SIMPLE MAN looking for someone to trust as much as I believe in myself, and not be deceived by the few lost souls whose hearts are harden and calculating from trusting one to many.

Just a SIMPLE MAN who has seen through the eyes and lives of others, and wants to do more for the forgotten, lost, misunderstood, and the outcasts and the rejects whose only crime is believing that there is no box but the one you create.

You see I am far from being rich and too informed to simply ask for wealth to fix it all. So, I lend you my ear and knowledge from past mistakes in hopes to reach just one…that will evade most of the mistakes that this SIMPLE MAN has made in the time given to him.

I want more than I believe time will allow me to complete, I am a SIMPLE MAN with dreams bigger than his wallet, hopes and imagination that cannot be quantified, reasoned, or determined by someone's doubt.

What makes me a SIMPLE MAN you see, is not faith, race, age, income, or pain but the fact that while I speak, you respond… and I know I'm not alone… because I still have your attention and I haven't lost my connection to those I have yet to reach.

CHILD OF THE SYSTEM #SPOKENTRUTH
THURSDAY, JUNE 25, 2015

I am the Child that the System forgot.

Prejudged from birth, because I was one of the have-not's.

The color of my skin, the place I grew up in, the people who I might call my friends, make me a statistic that should not be speaking to you young women and men.

You see, I was born to a single mother who used what she got from men that chose to fuck and lay instead of stay, so she learned just how to make them pay.

I am the Child that the System tried to stop. Told I was too fat, too black, too educated to give thought, until it was time for them to make a profit off a child who they took without thought.

At 14, my sister and I were whisked off and given new moms and pops.

At 18, I was free - dropped off and told *don't you fucking call, because we've washed our hands; we did our job to keep you out of a grave plot and all.*

At 19, my mother was murdered - brutally and savagely murdered - not a note, nor a call of condolence, so I just moved on from the System that told me they were far better than my mom.

At 25, I celebrated! I beat this fucked up System! This young man that was too fat, too black, too poor and now too well spoken...only had 1 child, no record, no bodies, not 6 feet under or locked behind prison doors.

The statistics, teachers, government officials, hood nor lifestyle did not take this Child of the System down the wrong road. So at 30, I started to speak and give my thoughts on the System… no longer a Child lost in the System, but a man who sees through it and learned to fight within it.

Radio, T.V, spoken word, writing books, global newspapers, social media.... I can cook, build, and inspire others through activism!!!

So, middle finger to the air, because this Child of the System will not be stopped! My revolution will be live and socialized, not televised… and I am sure to give you thought.

Unrivaled
February 18, 2015

Sidetracked, sidelined, and damn near derailed, my fate has so many tales to tell.

I must be gifted because I will not fail.

Mountains of failure, seas of doubt, so I will take to the sky and leave my fears to pout.

My heart, mind and soul are ready to do the things that are only in my dreams.

I shall let my inner voice shout and never be muffled by those without curiosity, imagination, or the heart to believe… as long you're here, your work has only just begun.

I prepare for war and gut up! No chapter of my life has been easy but this one is mine and I will be fine.

Is It Me You Seek?
FRIDAY, APRIL 8, 2016

I am a man.

Broad shoulders, strong back, undying will, courageous and strong.

King of his household, that only bows down to his queen.

I will defeat any enemy you put up against me.

If you cut me emotionally, I do bleed -- but with that crimson blood from my pumping emotional heart, I will use as Ink to write you out of history and into oblivion where you belong.

For I am a brute strong and unscathed from physical pain, but articulate still the same.

My words are far more powerful than my fists, and do damage that cannot be erased.

Reflection in the Mirror
FRIDAY, SEPTEMBER 9, 2016

My Great grandmother was a Blackfoot.

My great, great grandfather was a Slave Owner.

You only see the skin I am in; but the battles I have dealt with my whole life you will never know.

Until you look beyond my color and see my soul within.

I Am A Poet #SpokenTruth
MONDAY, JUNE 13, 2016

You see I am poet, now everyone knows it.

I can no longer deny my Spoken Truth. My words are like cocaine, mainstreamed directly into your brain, dealing blows and hits that no one can dismiss.

You can duck, dodge, dance, and weave but, hell, I never miss.

My words are like a three-piece combo… that hit heart, mind, body and soul with lyrics and verse that would have Maya Angelo weeping at the story that is about to be told.

Spoken Truth is what I do, exposing the world and people just like you to the unspoken truths that are simply dismissed because we are taught from birth that not one person can stop the unspeakable crimes mankind has let loosed on a world that would rather sit at home, watch T.V, play on their motherfucking phones, be fed lies, half-truths, and told what to do.

But, you see, I am living proof… I have faced every obstacle and distraction set before me, dead set on living my spoken truth.

So, I'll grab the mic, stage, or anywhere just so I can inspire you.

I know I won't be here forever, but I'm searching for those people, those chosen few that also see the truth and want to leave this world just a little bit better than what we were berthed into.

You see I'm a poet and at the end of Spoken Truth...yes, even I know it.

Blind Cries, Broken Speech
MONDAY, NOVEMBER 21, 2016

Hello world, this is Spoken Truth.

Can you feel me there... moving up your spine? Through books, pages, and poetry that will last the test of time.

Have I engorged your senses and tickled your mind? Gently kissed the folds, caressed those lost memories and scars behind your eyes.

Leaving etchings of truth with imagery so focused, poignant, soul shattering and true.

Don't feel some type of way if you haven't met me yet, see you already know me...

I'm that voice of regret, joy, pain, love, loss, and respect... that we try and push away so we can make it through our days, shifting from one mask to another as we try to live better days.

Now I leave that bittersweet cornucopia on your tongue, across your lips and skin...

As I let my morning start its daily run and begin all over, till the end.

Silent Thoughts
MONDAY, NOVEMBER 21, 2016

There are moments that I can never share.

Memories that are no longer there.

Places and events that seem to whisper into thin air.

I have no goal to where I'm going, no set destination for the things I need to see.

If you choose to follow me, always remember to move your feet.

No longer grounded by the normal, because life is all around me.

Who Am I?
SATURDAY, FEBRUARY 4, 2017

I have cried more tears than anyone will ever know. Been in more pain than one soul should know. I've seen so much death and destruction my eyes will not close... nah, this ain't poetry; it's my life untold.

I lost everything I cherished before age 25, but I kept pushing on so that teacher will know... I survived and did not die... nah, this ain't poetry; it's my life untold.

I've witnessed the most beautiful things and lived the most tragic tales. I've scared demons back into their decrepit crypts with just one touch. I've been broken, beaten, betrayed, and left for dead... nah, this ain't poetry; it's my life untold.

I've tasted the sweetest fruit and swallowed the most bitter of pills. I've inspired the youngest and oldest souls by letting my Truth be shown. My smile is my armor that has no weakness. I have more scars than unseen skin, more memories forgotten by legions of friends... nah, this ain't poetry; it's my life untold.

When I stop smiling, don't bother to call your friends, because you're on the wrong end of eyes that no longer consider you my friend... nah, this ain't poetry; it's my life untold.

Gravity
TUESDAY, NOVEMBER 22, 2016

I am completely unaware of the gravity of my own life...

As I orbit in the space provided to me, shifting layers of skin, friends, family, places, and lifetimes of memories.

I am completely unaware of the gravity of me...

Constantly moving towards goals unknown, picking up pieces of friends and strangers who are either sucked in or thrown out by the gravity I do not see.

I am completely unaware of the gravity others see...

The sheer terror, torment, happiness, pain, joy, devotion, carelessness, hope and misery far outside the reach of this unseen entity, forever circling their own destiny.

I am only aware of the gravity that I feel when... I speak...

Moving, hearts, minds, bodies and souls to the rhythm of my hypnotizing speech. Flowing effortlessly through the movements of their minds, piercing oceans of gravity at limitless speeds searching for the conscience that only sees................................Me.

What Is Spoken Truth?   #SpokenTruth
MAY 16, 2016

What is Spoken Truth?

Spoken Truth is wordplay so beautiful, so inspiring, so pure, so honest, and so true I will make your soul cry even if I never meet you.

Now I'm a storyteller, so every word and every verse that I write and perform is meant to inspire something new within you.

So come with me, this mad-hatter, as I take you down my yellow brick road to never-never land where all my dreams shall be told.

As I tell you about my life through learning, love, pain, activism, joy and strife… you will be there with me as I bring these words to life.

Now, this might sound like poetry or spoken word to many of you, but it's really just the thoughts in my head that I have only told a chosen few.

Now, I let you see behind the veil and all the things I seem to do so well, in hopes that I will inspire just a few…

Through my own public view.

SPOKEN
TRUTH

Chapter 2

> Bridges do not ask for a *thank you*…they are simply happy to see you get to the other side – J. Summers

…Things My Father Never Told Me

Dead Silence/No Justice, No Peace #SpokenTruth
December 5, 2014 at 11:58pm

If you stand for nothing, you'll fall for anything. I like this and I believed it for many years… until everything in my life caused me to skew this image just a bit.

If you stand for nothing, everything will change - certain things you do and stand for only makes them remain the same.

It's not about being a follower or even a leader anymore; it's about what change comes about when someone screams your name. Trayvon Martin, Michael Brown, Eric Garner, Aiyana Jones, Tamir Rice, Freddie Gray, John Crawford, Sandra Bland, Aaron Pope, Emmett Till!!!

Our communities are drowning, flooded with images of being a bad bitch, a dancer, a dope boy, or an instant celebrity from World Star, Face Book, Instagram, Twitter, or Snap Chat; for what?

It seems like no one sees the damage they do to the youth growing up.

All the images of money, needless things to buy, senseless violence, relationships with no fucking sense of pride and people condemned to die… really seems to be the new form of enslavement.

It's not just one specific race or one specific people/it's happening all around....

(Continued)

(Continued)

While you look at your phone, tablet, or the latest piece of technology they throw in front of you, you are being taught to forget how to communicate with the person in front of you.

We're being raped intellectually and we don't even care.

Don't drink the water! Ebola is coming!, ISIS and Trump are at your front door!, and *Black Lives Matter!* (as they should to all). But we have done more damage to our own people, our own history, our own culture, children, souls and all than any police officers call!!!

Until we can all stand united without race, religion, income, background, or social fucking status, then our whole species is destined to fall!!!

The school system is in state of disarray; no art, no music, no transportation, no books, and no sports to play.

While legation rewrites history and calls it fact, because we have another war to win over the horizon and I bet you that's a fact.

We are taught to believe *no new friends*, don't trust them, but find a way to get ahead and make a difference - just don't do too much… or you'll find yourself left for dead for 4 hours with 47 bullets or stalked and choked inside your jail cell instead.

NO JUSTICE, NO PEACE; HANDS UP, DON'T SHOOT; I CAN'T BREATHE! But I will speak until there is no more breath in my lungs to speak to see my people's minds, bodies, and souls released from these evil beasts.

As I sip my little sip
September 9, 2013

As I sit here and sip on my little bottle, I feel lost alone in the abyss of my own heart.

My friend and me, until you're gone as well.

Kill the pain of rejection even if it's just for the moment.

My eyes only see what they cannot have - blinded by the tears of a love lost never to be returned.

Alone in a world with a god that doesn't answer and people who are only out for themselves, forked tongues that spread the most beautiful lies and weave the most intricate webs of deceit and betrayal.

My friend and me; dilute the pain and dismal part of my life until you are also gone leaving me here wanting, yearning to give what I have to offer…so much within me, but for most it's only second best.

Oh what joy I would have to find someone that wants me for me, and not because I am the only one around, but she wants to.

I don't ask for much… just to share my life with someone that wants to give as much as I do.

My friend soothes my restless nights; alone I lay till my body gives out and sleep takes me till the next day.

As I sit here and sip on my little bottle.

This City That I Come From #SpokenTruth
MARCH 30, 2016

This city that I come from...

This city that I come from...'T-Town, 419, The Glass, Frog Town, The Mud, Holy Toledo Better Watch Your Ass' sprouts so much attention, controversy, and doubt over the people within and the crimes we only tell our friends... about our water, politics, roads, nightclubs, public housing, school system and people who really ought to just be friends.

This city that I come from… has so much murder and senseless death from cousins killing cousins and people that didn't know each other until they saw their family getting dressed.

This city that I come from…has so much potential and new growth but very few see that because they want their pockets to show them the path of new hope.

This city that I come from...

This city that I come from……'T Town, 419, The Glass, Frog Town, The Mud, Holy Toledo Better Watch Your Ass' truly is my home; it's like no other place that I have been on my own... home of the $5 bag for $4 (and you know we had to get Rello's). Promotors that don't even show up no more (because at their last 4 shows no one was at the door). Women that are just as bad as men when you tell them you only want to be their friend (so they run around town telling lies and convincing people of how you mistreated them). People who will tell you a dragon's tail if only to make a sale (and you know if you buy 12). And if you don't like the weather, just wait a day or two. (We go from sun to hail, from snow to rain then sun again -- and believe me my friend that is true).

(Continued)

(Continued)

This city that I come from…if you go right outside your area code you learn the most interesting stuff...this city that I come from has heart, art, soul, beautiful and inspiring stuff... sports teams, museums, parks, libraries, artists you never knew existed whose voice, music, and talent will have your souls lifted....Art Tatum, Jamie Farr, and many more were born here!

This city that I come from…the museums are magnificent; we have an amazing Zoo, beautiful parks, mind opening libraries and talented artists in every form that ever existed... from glass, to portrait, to building and skin, orchestra, solo artists, dancers, T.V, actors, video/radio/print. Around every corner there is a story you never knew could be true about people that gave their life to see others survive and wanted no fame or glory, but just know they've paid their price… in blood, sweat, tears, and pain so that another could see another day without pain from blame.

This city that I come from...
This city that I come from…'T-Town, 419, The Glass, Frog Town, The Mud, Holy Toledo Better Watch Your Ass' is just one man's point of view, but I hope that I painted a decent picture for you,

… My name is J Summers, Child Of The System…and all I do is Spoken Truth.

City Crimes, A Mother's Cries, And Young Men Die! #SpokenTruth
THURSDAY, APRIL 7, 2016

We are trapped in cities where no one gives a fuck... babies killing babies and a mother's screams just ain't enough... Cops gone insane and dope boys pulling rank while blind eyes are everywhere but mouths, fingers, and hearsay run marathons to tell the case...

We have a problem going on and your phone, TV and complaints won't fix it today... You talk about poppin' bottles and fucking models or how you have the streets on lock, but none of that's going to save you when your boy or an officer pulls a glock... then puts you six feet under and now your baby's screaming: *Daddy's been shot*!

Even if you miss that sightless bullet, you'll wind up behind bars where nobody gives a fuck cuz now the government has paid for you stay in concrete walls, surrounded by cemetery blocks of your fellow soldiers who claimed they couldn't be stopped!

You better listen up cuz this might be your last shot… Justice or Else!... take some of that rage and learn how to build for yourself, because at the end of the day, you will wind up another name on a tee-shirt that will fade and the memory of you will be used as another young youth takes a bullet to the grave!

You can sit up and say no one cares or that nothing will ever change; but I have been to the murder sites and I have seen the families' pain before they had to put their loved ones down six feet to fill up an empty grave… and still they remain dealing with their pain doing their best to inspire change. At the cost of everyone else telling them you're just gonna lose yourself, because we just came to be on TV and fucking social media like everyone else!!!!!

Motivation #SpokenTruth

MONDAY, JUNE 20, 2016

You see you may think you know me, but there's way more to be seen.

Now, while I might be an educated man speaking poetry, performing, and fighting for other people's dreams; I live in the hood, yes, I live in the hood where I go to sleep to terrible things… gunshot fire, sirens, drunken arguments, babies crying, and railcars screeching.

Police roll by in gangs of bikes, just so they can profile you and send their vehicles to take away your rights. Their patrol cars weave through the cell blocks that we try to make our homes, wrecking kids' toys that have been left outside till the owners come home.

I live in the hood… I wake up to yellow taped murder scenes, banging on the door, and loud music outside my window till I can't take it anymore. You see my alarm clock is the screaming children left all alone, while the lawn mower crew works 6 days a week constantly leaving their equipment running while they chase after something sweet. No parents in sight and then mothers begin to fight over a daddy that is not there because he's out getting some pipe from a man he claims to be his *'boi'*.

I live in the hood…where if you steal, lie, and cheat you are crowned King. But I haven't always lived here, and I don't plan on staying here. I've seen too much of the world and I have lived in beautiful places, far away and free from fear and theft because someone else has less. I live in the hood…living here takes strength no screenwriter could make up, for actors to play pretend or for mixtape sales generations.

Yes, it will take some getting used to - waking up to little kids playing, the sound of nature as it exists outside the hood without gunshots raining but, rather, listening to the sounds of peace and quiet, enjoying playtime with my little girl before she's all grown up and doesn't need daddy for entertainment.

I live in the hood…and out of all I do for everyone else, my daughter is the reason I will not stop doing my best to make sure she never sees this life that has caused me so much pain and stress. Even though it has not consumed me, it has taught me its valuable life lessons: your life can be gone at any moment so, people, please - can we put down the guns and stop second guessing?

Stolen Memories

TUESDAY, NOVEMBER 22, 2016

There you are my good friend Stress… just when I think you're gone and I can finally take a breath...

You tap me on the shoulder, reminding me of the things I have yet to complete, the promises I've made to myself and others, and the journey still ahead...

I share you with no one but myself; you're my little secret, always keeping a smile on my face where you rest...knowing none can handle you but me. I take others' pain as if I am a black hole that can never be satisfied or find comfort in rest...

My friend is mine, not to share or give - at least I pray I don't because of someone else's unrest...

Always reminding me of where I have been, will go, and what can never be taken back...

So once again I give you to my Creator, hoping for peace and enlightenment till the next time I open my eyes seeing all that has been kept.

20 to Life #SpokenTruth
THURSDAY, DECEMBER 8, 2016

The Block Don't Need You!

Trap houses will go on just in a different form, co-sponsored by the pharmacy, government, and the majority of those who gave up on you. All to keep our children blind to their true crowns and knowledge. We are all destine to drown if we don't feed our future leaders now!

The blood you spilled, those stripes you earned, the plug y'all robbed, and the multiple women you've burned just to hang them like trophies while your seeds continue the only cycle they've ever learned!

That won't mean SHIT when your family is selling dinners and begging strangers to help bury you! All because your boi, bae, plug, baby momma, and closest family just robbed you while you flat line in the street or a hospital bed with no one around you!

Don't fall into that trap! **The Block Don't Love You!**

The block only wants every ounce of blood from you! The block wants your children to grow up in poverty with you! The block wants every generation you birth to stack with no growth, to spread disease with no hope, to preach but not teach, to eat and not feed... while we kill our Kings and Queens over land we don't own!

The Block Needs you to Never Have a Voice. It needs you to feed the statistics that say *you all belong in cages and in chains*, surrounded by walls for society to throw down like used tissues; to be surrounded by the usual – "We Miss You", "FREE MY BOO", Teddy Bear poled pictures, RIP T-Shirts, whilst they say, "That's not our issue, and here's our proof".

SOCIETY IN DISTRESS
April 6, 2015 at 3:18pm

I have heard, seen, and have done many things. My thoughts on this, I guess, are little bit cloudy… after all this time alone watching so many relationships go so wrong.

The whole damsel in distress/knight in shining armor dilemma as I have witnessed it from my own eyes.

For those women that claim they're a damsel in distress and are waiting on their knight in shining armor, I just have a few questions.

Are you really ready for your knight in shining armor? Have you taken care of your own insecurities, disbeliefs, and doubt about this man who has come to save you.

Are you ready to give away some of your control and be the woman he's been fighting so hard to save, or is it that you just need someone to carry some of the baggage while you continue searching for *you*.

When you gaze upon him with his blunted blade, dented shield, and mangled armor will you tell him (as many others have done before): I'm not ready to be free… just yet?

For all those wayward knights in shining armor, is your own castle secure? Before you step off your throne and armor up, preparing to fight the demons, insecurities, unpacked bags, and possibly a lifetime of doubt, do you have all the necessary requirements to take care of not only yourself, but also the Queen that you bring back, she who is your dream?

As you gaze upon your damsel/your future queen with her hidden scars, mountain of regrets, and unmarked grave, of all the ones that came before you with lies so sweet but still they chose to move their feet, will you tell her (as all the ones before you) that your heart cannot give her peace?

Devil's Walk
SEPTEMBER 9, 2016

***

Fear of the unknown leads to anger.

Anger causes pain; pain leaves you empty and alone.

Stand in front of the darkness and create your own light, and never fear the path ahead.

The fear is only in your head.

***

Freedom Fighter
FEBRUARY 4, 2017

Leaders are not born; they are created by the mass of people that believe in them, who see their ability not to quit.

Heroes are created by the death of the fallen few, whose undying will remains in the hearts of all of you, keeping fires blazing for generations to come.

Every last one of them were human beings who could not just watch someone else being abused.

SPO
TRUTH
My
Words

Chapter 3

> If you are always upset about being rubbed the wrong way… how will you ever be polished? – J. Summers

…Random Thoughts

My Foundation
APRIL 12, 2016

I trusted you!

You have been there with me since the beginning - always strong, flexible, and dependable.

You've never given me a reason to doubt you every time I needed you. You were always there on long walks, mountain climbs, being chased in the dark, keeping me stable when I thought I couldn't go on.

All the games we have played and places we've been – the care that I showed you I know wasn't the best... sometimes I pushed you too far and didn't give you much rest. Yes, I could have rubbed you those nights you probably were in distress.

How was I supposed to know you were at your breaking point? You took everything in stride and made me believe inside there wasn't anything I couldn't do without you by my side.

I trusted you; on that fateful day you decided to separate and leave me black and blue causing me pain and embarrassment that I have never knew. As I lie on the ground with no one to help - and now they all look at you.

Now you want me to trust you as I did before saying, "I'm sorry, I'll be stronger than I was", and "you'll never have to question me again, I'll keep your feet on the floor."

Well my trust doesn't come easy - but I need you and I can't replace you.

Only now there is fear of what you might do if I piss you off, knowing I can't take another fall.

So, I guess I will have to trust you because you are my knee and all. Thanks for listening about how I dislocated my knee because that was quite a fall ;-)

Just Thinking

February 28, 2017

Throughout my life I've had misfortunes, pitfalls, re-start after re-start; but I've also had great heights.

Miraculous things have happened to me that gave me such joy in a short period of time.

The moments I was in despair became obsolete. To be honest, if I had not gone through so much pain and suffering I would not be able to understand you.

I would not know how to relate to the things you can't escape, see your tears and fears, those not thought about in years.

Without pain, I would not have learned to be so concerned about the thoughts you dare not think and dream, nor do you speak.

Living a life overshadowed by sex, lies, and greed.

Maybe it's me, maybe I do not see what you see and maybe I've become so blinded by my loss, my life of pain… that has brought me to such a claim.

Where everyone is a victim, and no one is free of pain.

Sleepless Thoughts
SEPTEMBER 9, 2016

When you are born into a country that stole its land from a native race.

Reminded daily by the color of your skin, how your people were enslaved,
brainwashed, and displaced.

It's hard not to be filled full of rage, anger, and hate.

But I just keep a smile on my face and look forward to the day,
when we all realize
we're the entire human race.

Going To Bed
NOVEMBER 21, 2016

I was going to post, but I'm going to bed.

It has been a great day with only one stress.

I have work in the morning and I need my rest.

I'll be back in a few to terrorize my loose-lipped naysayers with tonight's
success, but I need to get my rest.

Lots on my mind and there isn't enough time to share what I'm really going
through, so I am taking my ass to bed.

Blah...Blah

NOVEMBER 21, 2016

I would not post, if I did not do so much...

If I did not post, I would not do so much...

This has been bothering me for quite some time now...

26 Letters

February 28, 2017

26 letters of Grand Design.

I used to work any story, genre, and design.

Created and crafted from the memories of my mind.

Let me tell you a story where every word will be true, illustrated in the minds and hearts of all of you.

Specifically targeted to spark the imagination you never knew, because every story is unique, including you.

Head Games

February 28, 2017

Fear nothing, go everywhere.

Make memories not just with your eyes, but your soul.

If you let man-made borders and barriers control your destiny,

You will only go as far as the imaginary control.

A Note to My Muse
March 1, 2017

I would like to say hello to you, my beautiful, inspiring, dream crafting, soul quenching Muse.

We have known each other since high school, although I do not remember those days as you do.

You are there with me in my mind, inspiring these 26 letters of Grand Design. Allowing me to create and give voice to the words that could only come from my mind.

I thank you for the energy you send my way; the vibrations from others just don't feel the same.

Even though our universes are parallel, destined to never intermix, exchange a star or two and match.

I am pleased when they do cross paths, if only for a glimpse...

To see the moon, stars, oceans of memories, and beautiful summer that is you.

No names needed, you know who you are.

That's just how the universe works... she may never read her note.

Life I Left Behind
March 1, 2017

I am beginning to miss club life - this is not good.

It gave me something to do, and now I'm just up not able to sleep
.

Hopefully this too will pass...or I'm going to wind up getting a job
again.

I never did it for the money, people, or to have a good time.

It was a way for me to clear my mind, surrounded by memories of
pcople I barely knew who gathered together because of music, food,
dancing, and promises of something new.

Hey, stop reading my journal! I didn't write this for you...nah, I'm just
fucking with you. I'm bored…with nothing else to do.

Good Afternoon
March 1, 2017

Good afternoon to you.

Well, it's time for me to get off this couch; I really must leave this house.

I have bills to pay and people to see, ideas to inspire and dreams of better things.

So, it's time that I got out of this house; nobody but me to accomplish the things that I need, to make sure I don't wind up on somebody else's couch.

I must stop looking at this screen which sits here and devours me while 'life' is outside of my house.

Nobody to blame but me myself if I do not put my phone down and get out of this house.

Sleep can put a lot of things into perspective, like all those emotions that you thought you had just a few hours ago or that thing you misplaced that was staring you in the face.

You just need a moment of rest to clear your mind and *Let It Go*. You'll find it once you recharge and your batteries are no longer low.

Anyway, I'm up; I always have a lot to do but that's just routine for me.

I've been moving forward for so long I honestly forget to look back to see what I've done. I get that through all the people that I know, even though I talk about relationships a lot but don't we all on some level? You are either in one, searching for one, no longer comfortable, or without one.

I know my writing does not have the correct punctuation most of the time, but it's not something you have to buy or spend any unnecessary time on. If you do not want to read, please don't criticize me.

Here you're talking to *me,* not an auto-correct. I know <u>what</u> I said, or at least I know <u>what I meant.</u>

(Continued)

(Continued)

Well this is getting a lot longer than I wanted it to be, so I will say this: My life has always been stuck in one gear, moving forward… through obstacles, walls, barriers, oceans, mountains, gravity, and death. My side view mirrors are very small and I rarely use the rear view.

My 'vehicle' did not come equipped with turn signals, so I just have to take my chances.

If you decide to become a passenger with me as we take this journey called life, please buckle up, grab the stick shift - but be gentle - and remind me when it's time to hit the brake.

You are well protected though; the tread is reinforced by all those that closed their doors, the windows and doors are all armor plate manufactured by this twist of fate called my life.

You can even pick the radio station if you like, as we move on down the road.

There's plenty of storage space, cuz I keep no baggage of my own....

Just a little blue box by the spare that I used to call my home.

Room for passengers and yes, your family must come too.

I don't know where the road ends, but I would be happy to find it with you.

I'm done, that's how most of my poems actually start out.
I started out thinking one thing and then.. history.

Enjoy.

Future phone calls

JUNE 3, 2016

Hello, I just wanted to say much love to you, and no matter how far I go away from the guy you once knew that is off to see better days, I'm just phone call away.

Honestly, I have something I need to get off my chest.

You can call me if you want and, yes, I will answer. Stop blaming me if I am the only one who speaks, claiming I have a phone that receives because all I see is *send* and *not received* on the other end of my phone when we speak.

So, go ahead call me up, I don't hold grudges, but just know this… if I don't start to see a receive on the other end of my screen, you're probably somebody I should not call my friend on the other end of this conversation when we speak.

Now just hold up, don't get all pumped up, I'm just letting you know, the interest that you show in me being your friend.

See I'm just reciprocating the feeling from a true friend, who would like you around for more than a phone call when everything in your life starts to fall down.

So anyways how was your day? Anything new…is there a problem only I can solve for you?

Hello, hello, are you there? Why so quiet? You normally have a lot to say. I hope I didn't just ruin your day, because I'm only being a friend giving you the good with the bad, like a friend is supposed to -- being true to you, while being real with me.

CLICK. Hello, hello I guess we really were not that close.

SPOKEN
TRUTH

Chapter 4

Stop letting people gain polish off your grind. The smallest pebble was once a mighty mountain holding back the wind, water and earth. Until the cycle of life turned it back into earth, to be protected as it had been for others. The most impressive Oak started off as a meager seed nourished by a life no one lives to see. – J. Summers

...Seasonal Love

The Search for Peace of Mind Continues
September 5, 2013

My goal is to penetrate your mind not your body.

As our heartbeats slowly sync to become one, we are no longer just two people that fate gave a chance to meet.

Soon our souls will become intertwined to a point where you and I fade until there will only be us.

Our individual goals past, present and future will blend until the outside world only thinks of us not as a parasitic bond, but a symbiosis union that has no end or beginning.

Just The Tip #SpokenTruth
December 8, 2014

I've met a few women that broke the surface, even one that took a swim - but not one yet that was willing to truly let me be with them.

I know she's out there - one day we will meet. But until then, I shall continue to move my feet.

I have no time for games, one night stands, what if's, or maybes - let it be real or 'peace to you' baby.

I understand on the surface I shine and amaze, polished by the grinding stone of life and age, while the true depths of me remains fractured, misshapen, unseen, and enraged. Long ways down these memories go, but only my queen will know what I know.

Sweetest Kiss #SpokenTruth
March 8, 2015

Kiss me so softly, so deeply, so long so that all others are routinely dismissed.

I need passion, intimacy, ecstasy, and bliss.

Take me to that place where only you and I exist.

Kiss me, but not just a kiss.

Make me yearn, make me tremble, make me quiver, hunger, want, weak and need from just from that kiss.

Show me why it's you that I should share my lips.

Set my soul on fire, ignite my desire… from the moment our lips touch tip to tip.

22 Days
May 2, 2014

From the moment it started, I had a gut feeling this was too good to be true.

Like most things in my life, they start with a large explosion of released, untapped energy.

However, as with anything that burns too quickly, the speed of ignition soon forces them to implode upon themselves.

I must say, in this short span of time every range of emotion has been felt at nearly the speed of light - blink and you missed it.

This experience has left me spent, not in the sense I can't go on…never that, but it will be a good while before I give that much of myself to anything or anyone with a loose foundation.

I've learned a lot in this short span of time that I could not have learned if I did not choose to divert the path I was on.

New journeys lay ahead…the part of me that was still naive to certain elements of this world are now fully mature.

All that's left of me now is to choose which fork, in my twisted rubix cube path of life, I will take.

I have taken both paths before, but never with so much on my back. I've always traveled light whenever I hit a crossroads in my life.   This time is very different. Although the easy way seems logical, I know myself and without a few twists, unlit trails, potholes, and dead ends I will not feel challenged.

I am ready to see what the next chapter in my life holds - the anticipation is killing me.

In Need Of #SpokenTruth

March 29, 2015

I am in need of, and not just a want of, that person to be mine so we should never want.

Not just for the season, experience, or loops in my belt, but to be mine. And, if I am hers, we will play with the cards we are dealt.

I am in need of my partner, my equal, my challenger, my believer, my rock - so we can stop entertaining all those without thought.

I am in need of the one to understand that I am just a man, not fiction…who will probably make mistake after mistake, but never keep me far from thought, never tarnish what I want for us because of something plush.

I am in need of someone that understands reality as I do, even if it's seen through the eyes of you…someone to play, someone to lay, someone to build with! Someone who is tired of all the games people play.

I am in need of no more promises of giving me all the glory while you empty yourself…please don't forget your own story... if this is about me and you, then let me explore you and erase all lessons of misuse.

Let's breathe life into one another, till our souls have no cover, no shade, and no escape - just naked as we embrace. We will pierce each other's mind, body, and soul as we peel back the layers of miseducation taught to us by all those wayward souls.

I am in need of trust, honesty, loyalty, and respect; but most of all, understanding…because both of us have been taught the price you pay when you're too eager to hear the words *I Love You* and forget your last loss and all the mistakes that were made.

To be vulnerable, to give completely - neither one of us wants to be lost. Soul searching is not easy and completely impossible if you are both lost.

I'm in need of the one who has been through the hurt, the pain, and the rejection of a fairytale that only sits to grow moss, while everyone else just sits around bumping and running into each other as if they were all just programmed rocks!

I am in need of you to be there… not just sit there as we push and pull and tug upon one another…it's an equal battle we'll face each day as we learn to love one another.

Illicit Dreams #SpokenTruth
JANUARY 30, 2015

As he spreads her legs, he sees life within.

His rod at full attention, until she lets him in.

Life standing still, till they can become one.

Pressure mounting energy building for the moments of soul play that will soon the end.

Let's escape into each other, take a swim, and dive deep, no reason for air… let's explode on one another in this moment we share.

Cupcake #SpokenTruth
DECEMBER 31, 2015

The first day I saw you -

I thought I knew where my life was headed. I had goals, dreams, aspirations, a bright future, and I damn sure was invested…but you changed that.

I saw you and you saw me - NAKED, VENERABLE, and INCOMPLETE.   There was no WALL, no SHEILD, no EGO, and no past PAIN that could be CREATED to hide how we felt about one another each and every day.

I was so scared; you PIERCED every bluff, every attempt to dismiss simply with a word, a glance, a touch, or *baby you are missed*…and I was helpless and convinced, knowing you were MY ONE.

The day that we KISSED.... My entire life flashed before me and in that instant, I knew I was complete; I knew that my fruitless search for peace of mind had finally come to an end. I had to slap myself every day I woke up just to be sure I wasn't still ASLEEP… that this QUEEN lying next to me wasn't just another DREAM, another FANTASY, FAIRYTAILE, or NIGHTMARE - because you were everything I NEEDED.

We said I LOVE YOU and my heart should have BURST right out of my chest and ran off into another universe, but instead we were the LOCK and KEY that gave each other SECURITY and PEACE.

Traveling around the country seeing things we'd NEVER seen, doing things we'd never DREAMED… changing history while EXPOSING the world to YOU and ME. There were long nights we'd just sit and talk about all of our FEARS, TEARS, HISTORY, SOUL, DREAMS, and FUTURE until we were both at ease knowing we were each other's future. Passing out to the SUNRISE - holding each other tight knowing we would see our own living DREAM consisting of you and I later on that night.

I write, perform, protest, and speak on things that people push away. You illustrate everything that people didn't know could be SEEN that way.

My LOVE, for you were an ETERNAL FLAME that would have never FADED because we FUELED each other every day with HOPE that no ONE could have ever taken our special place.

Let Me

March 17, 2015

Let me heal the wounds and scars within; don't hide behind your chained heart again.

Let me teach you to trust again - I will not fail you nor will I stray; just let me be the only one you can't keep away.

Let us explore each other and get to know one another not just for passion, but for intimacy way beyond the physical limitations of our bodies' vulnerability.

Let me know you as I know me; give me something to work for but please don't just give me the key.

Let us free our minds as our bodies and souls intertwine, making music with each other as if it's our first time.

Let me be there for you when you feel everything is wrong and nobody belongs.

Let me wipe away the tears and fears of long forgotten lovers and prove to you, to us, there is no other.

Let me be the one to unravel all the lies they've spun, and show you that you are the one to be treasured and pleasured until the morning sun.

Let us begin a new phase/chapter 2 - and let all the hurtful trash of the past be used to fuel the things we will never do.

I give you me, you give me you -- let us be renewed.

Catcher's Mitt
NOVEMBER 21, 2016

A thoughtful moment………

Last month I blinked twice; when I opened my eyes I saw you standing there.

Every fiber of me wants to question why I am not afraid, but I will take this moment without question knowing you just kept me from going insane.

Finding peace and sweet release within your embrace.

Repeated Dreams
NOVEMBER 21, 2016

Wanting just a few more hours with you.

At least I got to rest with no regrets. Enjoying sweet memories of you, letting my mind do nothing else.

Long days…lonelier nights.

I'm working hard to provide a better future so all we have are playful nights, memories to make, and days with nothing but the best.

Rebound
NOVEMBER 22, 2016

We started off as something new, rebounding from those who claimed to be true.

Simple texts, inboxes, a call or two.

Then a photo, and *I miss you*, and a call that would change every wrong word spoken by the person who couldn't be true to you.

With a few kisses in special places, then waking up next to you, I decided it would be worth the chance I took with you.

We both knew of the feelings left behind from the person who wasted your time, and that you might rebound out of fear of something new. I take full responsibility for not paying attention to the signs that y'all were not completely through.

The passion was great in the moments that we could find time to play, whispering bright futures that are now distant memories.

At least I can say I was happy and at peace in those days, when you wanted to try to please me the right way.

But he saw his chance and finally decided he wanted to be your man – pulling rank by pulling history, heartache, and toys galore up to your heart's front door that I left unsecured.

I may want, need, and cherish the memory of you – I miss our circle of friends/family and time spent, but I will not play the fool.

A rebound for you I will be - at least you got your ring and to see the other side of things. You used your body as a tool for someone to truly care for you.

At least my heart never skipped a beat while I was thinking of you. Only now, the future I have ahead will have to be lived without you.

Goodbye Brea…thank you for the hard lesson,

Your *Rebound*

Finding The Driven #SpokenTruth
March 8, 2015

As of late, I keep running into these beautiful/intelligent, yet emotionally damaged-driven women.

Please don't take it personal, your scars are a thing of beauty. They show struggle, pain, and lessons learned from a time when you knew not much.

Another man's blessing that he just threw away - so I'll listen to you and I'll learn from you, but I'll keep my heart tucked away.

I know they say to find that one you must have an open heart, but I'm trying to find that one that cannot be torn apart.

I only need one queen to sit beside this king...the one that sees what is in front of her and will not let another steal our dreams.

The one who demands my time and attention to be hers and hers alone.

Not out of jealousy, insecurity, or because she demands a throne. But because she never wants her king, this king, to never be alone.

Hopelessly Yours
NOVEMBER 21, 2016

Falling quickly…

Even I can't write these answers...

Silently whispering to my heart: *Is it okay to let go?*

Keep making those vibrations only we can feel, so there can be only us.

As we glide across the memories of all those that tried to stifle us at our best…in the end proving we do deserve love.

Hope
NOVEMBER 21, 2016

Everyday feels like I am shedding new skin.

I no longer look for happiness, as I understand it to be an ethereal thing that finds you when you stop searching.

Each day I wake up not looking for the next goal to accomplish, knowing that I will serve my purpose as long as I follow my path.

I am letting my mistakes be the timber on which I will use the current to fly and see sights I've never seen before.

Just thinking about my peace of mind. Peace.

Losing Faith
NOVEMBER 21, 2016

I may be misunderstood – I'm too deep, too sweet, too freaky, or I don't make sense most of the time – but…I wanted to love you.

I had my heart locked up so tight and buried behind so many walls, that no one could see the scars behind each silent beat my heart made…but it wanted to love you.

I lost my breath when you said you wanted to be with me; my ears felt deceived, all thoughts became scattered, and my heart beat erratically wanting to clear out a space only for you.

My lips couldn't say *please don't hurt me; I'll be your escape and learn to love you the right way.*

The first day we kissed I knew I was in deep shit. The times we said good morning/good night, and the time we didn't give a fuck and got that 'quick fix'.

Waking up to your skin, your beautiful grin, every curve/every inch. The sound of your voice brought me to full attention like no one ever could and danced in my head till we spoke again, knowing I truly wanted to love you.

Then came the days that took much space; it was the voice of you, my queen, that was keeping me sane.

So, I made some mistakes trying to keep my lovely all day, because I can't believe this feeling… when I am near your embrace.

Scattered Beats No One See's

NOVEMBER 22, 2016

Beat pause, Beat pause, Beat pause.

Steady as she goes, anticipating every moment, repairing old wounds and scars - reinforcing those places that have never been touched. Steadily ticking keeping its pace with life.

Beat pause, Beat pause, Beat beat.

Another wound, another scar never to be seen again that is concealed in forced smiles and misplaced thoughts. Hurt that endures long nights and even longer days, trying to find the strength to not be weak again.

Beat pause, Beat pause, Beat stop.

Who are you? Beat, Beat, Beat, Beat, Beat...Skip, I don't have room to be hurt - don't touch there! That spot is reserved! How dare you have such Nerve! I don't want to feel again!

Beat pause, Beat pause, Beat skip.

Stop whispering those beautiful memories addressed to places you may not want to see, promising healing concern for my needs, bringing your own scars into the picture that no one has seen.

Beat pause, Skip beat pause, Beat calm.

First fight...Will I lose you? Think quickly! That felt right. Don't close off –don't shut out! Speak to your Queen - that link you made was genuine; it was true.

Beat, Beat, Beat, Beat...Response...Beat sync, Beat sync.

More late nights, caressing new thoughts of brighter days. Our very own special place...tender kisses to replace every tear that was left to burn and scare you from finding your true soul mate.

Beat peace, Beat peace, Beat relief.

Beat sync, Beat sync, Beat repeat, every Kiss, every Smile, every tender Touch, and Soul Penetrating Moment. Just know with every Beat we Sync, your Soul sings to me.

A Letter To You, Pt.1 - Searching For You #SpokenTruth
MARCH 17, 2016

I know you're out there, one day I hope we meet so we can finally be free of this endless dating routine and stop investing, inviting and sharing ourselves with people who wander off to become someone else's dream.

I hope we haven't met before while I was pouring my heart out to someone that just up and closed their door…and now you wait for me to stop making mistakes wasting time on people only want to take from your plate and have no real intentions to stay.

I do not know your name, your face, your past, your touch, your kiss, or your deepest darkest secrets, but I know you're out there because I'm nearly complete all except for your missing piece.

I have faced my demons and let my heart run rampant, only to be trampled on by women who didn't give two fucks in the end…so they left scars so deep only you will be able to see the true me.

I know you're out there because even though I have peace within me I dream about my future queen, the things we will share that no one else would care, but for you and me it's our air.

I know you're out there, the woman who is meant to be my queen - because no man can have a stable kingdom without the foundation, wisdom, guidance, and love of his future queen.

I know you're out there because I can love again. All those women I thought were my friends were just lessons to prepare me for the fake women who will foam at the mouth when they see us out, wanting what they'll never have and people who we just joke about.

I know you're out there, the woman that will only love me and never miss a beat – from sentiments of *good morning, I miss you, where are you, I love you, be safe, goodnight…* even if we can't see each other every night.

I know you're out there, and when we meet, I will not sweep you off your feet - and I will see you as you see me, knowing there's no other place we would rather be.

A Letter To You, Pt.2 - Thinking Of You #SpokenTruth
APRIL 25, 2016

I want to make you feel beautiful every day!

Not because I say it, not because I display it, but because you know it. Even when we are apart we are in each other's heart.

Two beats that have become synced and linked with each other, not out of passion, fashion or because of what others think.

But because we fell for each other so hard, so deep, so passionately… that our souls intertwined and became synced.

From the moment you saw the tears behind my smile, I knew you wouldn't let me drown in my own fears of thinking that I would never find someone who deserved the crown and ring that only belongs to my queen.

I will never leave you without a smile, even when we are at odds and can't see eye to eye because no one should have the option to give you second thought of how much you mean to me…even when we don't speak.

I will always be your ear when no one cares and be there for us no matter what I lose in the process. As long as I have you there is no earthly possession that would have any value if I lost you.

Those are just a few of the reasons that when we find each other I know we will be true to us, because through these letters, every word of proof that I write to you, I will make come true so that you know I love only you.

If You Decide To Say Hello #SpokenTruth
APRIL 7, 2016

If you decide to say hello just know I am NOT Captain Save-A-Hoe...

Now, this doesn't mean I won't listen to certain parts of your life that were quite difficult and keep you up at night. Hell, we all make mistakes and just want someone that can relate to or find someone who is at least is willing to reciprocate some form of affection for the life that they have not lived and only you experienced. Who may just want a glimpse to be on the other side of the scars that reside in your mind where no amount of haze, daze, or drunken rage can give you back the days before you had your sanity ripped away.

But, I do repeat sweetheart - I'm not Captain Save-A-Hoe...

While I would love to suture some of those stitches that I might have exposed, that you try to cover with makeup, hair, skin-tight clothes and, yeah, that new found pole in more ways than one. I do see your heart with its scars and good intentions, but I know that we could never truly be friends because I, myself, need someone that is going to heal my soul - not conceal my soul; the Queen that will never try and use me or confuse me with the man that stole her heart and froze it because he was only playing his part.

Now I know that might sound cruel, but there was a woman before you who said all the right things and who touched me just the right way. But in the end, she left without even saying a fucking word to me, but alas a text to say: *thanks for helping me and all you did, but you ain't shit and I'm better off without you even though I still fucking love you…*followed by another woman who said *I love your dick and the things it makes me do, but I'm married so can I have it without investment in that real relationship shit?*

So, no, I am not Captain Save-A-Hoe…

But we can be friends though; I'll tell you no secrets and you'll tell me no lies - until we decide to drift off and live other lives.

Then I won't be Captain Save-A-Hoe, I'll be someone you know.

So, sweetheart before I let you go and, yes, you know I'm not Captain Save-A-Hoe...one last question - what's your name though?

A Letter To You, Pt.3 - That Comfortable Feeling #SpokenTruth
MAY 16, 2016

I want that comfortable feeling back...

Not the let's screw and talk, go out to eat, see each other every now and then, and play games with each other's minds till neither one of us make sense.

I want that comfortable feeling back...

The one where we sit and talk about building a better me and you, while we use the time given to us to find ways to enjoy every moment before there is something to do.

I want that comfortable feeling back...

Now you're cute but, hell, I don't trust you so I'll string you along; hopefully that will change, but until then I'll keep several others in plain view just in case it doesn't work between me and you.

I want that comfortable feeling back...

The one where I am only comfortable being with you and everyone else is an invader trying to steal the secrets I only share with you, so we only say what needs to be said knowing nothing new can be as precious as our life…me and you.

I want that comfortable feeling back...

Not the argumentative fight to prove each other's love till we no longer do, stay with each other because we're scared of something new, then cheat and lose a friend in the process too.

I want that comfortable feeling back...

The one where we can just lay up and laugh till it hurts and fall asleep to each other's heartbeats - the only sound that makes us feel complete - then wake up to the half sleep face covered in drool then kiss you on your other cheek.

I want that comfortable feeling back…

And I hope that you do too; I will have it when I am with you.

SPOKEN TRUTH
My words only

Chapter 5

Life was never meant to be easy…you are here to learn, love, and respect your limitations and if you see your lessons, help the next soul out. – J. Summers

…Inspiration Through Life

Stardust
March 8, 2017

You are an enigma.

A mind-boggling combination of elements and ideas, powered by a nuclear reactor that has no expiration date as long as you take care of it.

You are a mixture of things so incomprehensible and unimaginable there has to be faith to believe you exist.

But you are Stardust; we all exist in this cosmic mix.

Much love…now go power your future!

Birdcage
March 8, 2017

Fear nothing, go everywhere, make memories not just with your eyes, but with
your soul.

If you let man-made borders and barriers control your destiny,

you will only go as far as the imaginary control. 

Champagne Dreams/Project Nightmares
JULY 18, 2016

Champagne dreams and project nightmares is all anyone sees.
When you say that your DREAMS don't involve SELFISH needs,
but, rather, in helping other PEOPLE who are in need.

Your HOPE should INSPIRE someone else to not just live for THEMSELVES;
people with MONEY, HATE, and GREED will try and make you feel that you
are less than COMPLETE.

Champagne dreams and project nightmares is all that is FED to the youth growing
up.
Brainwashing them to BELIVE that everyone has GIVEN UP.
WE are old and too busy FIGHTING over material stuff, so on the FUTURE they
lay hold.

Champagne dreams and project nightmares is all you really need to SUCCEED.
To pull yourself out of the MUD and leave behind the things that no one should
ever SEE other than in their DREAMS.

Venomous Snakes

OCTOBER 23, 2015

How have I survived amongst the venomous snakes?

Because I feel most comfortable knowing that their devilish gaze, forked tongues, and sharp teeth cannot sway me to do as they say.

Why do I play amongst the venomous snakes as they slither, crawl, and sneak - trying to get their way?

Because, their tempting full gaze does not phase me; my eyes only see the true outcomes not the illusions of things they offer my way. Their teeth cannot puncture my life worn skin. Truth is they could never be my friend. Their lies from their sweet forked tongues only wish my defeat. They can never bring me to my knees.

Why do the venomous snakes stay out of my way? Because my light shines too bright and my feet are too quick. If they tried to strike, their heads would be detached with the simple flick of my wrist.

Who are these venomous snakes?

They are the demons that dwell within that have lost all hope of ever doing something that doesn't benefit them only. They are the twisted and fractured souls who deceive and insight fear with poisonous speech that is only meant to bring you to your knees. The tricksters that couldn't see the dream if they were heavily sedated and placed where you can only live your dreams - they would hiss and cry in pain that they must be dismissed from this peaceful place and they would cry out: "I can only exist where people use their fists and dismiss all of their righteousness."

But do not be afraid of these venomous snakes, because your fear is what gives them power over everything you create.

Fuck you Failure #SpokenTruth
September 27, 2014

As I speed down my road of life, you are always there in the rearview mirror… reminding me of my mistakes, mishaps, misfortunes, and incomplete goals. **Fuck you Failure!**

No matter what achievements, accolades or barriers I break through, you stay as a constant reminder. **Fuck you Failure!**

After the lights go off and the crowd dissipates, you stick around like an inescapable residue…a tarnish that most see and believe to be my shine but, in reality, you are a glow that none will ever understand but me. **Fuck you Failure!**

But what you fail to realize is that you will always be in the rearview… because I will never stop moving forward. I will never give up on my hopes, dreams, and bright future ahead so… **Fuck you Failure!**

I am a King! A god amongst the doubtful disbelievers and naysayers who would only wish for me to run out of gas, turn around, or slow down just a bit so they can catch up quite quickly…but aww *Hell Naw*! **Fuck you Failure!**

Fuck you Failure. I will always hold my head up high knowing you did not defeat me yet once again. I may have the scars that most will never see but your loss and defeat is what keeps me moving forward.

Fuck you Failure… really you are my friend in the end because when I am all alone you remind me of closed **DOORS** that should never be reopened. You remind me of old **PATHS** and **BRIDGES** that will forever remain **SCORCHED** and **BURNT** because I was too impatient, too head strong, too confident, too proud, and too **IGNORANT** to listen to reason.

The more I think about it, I should say, **Thank you Failure!** Because you're building a better me, **NUT** and **BOLT,** piece by piece. But no! My tank is on full and there's no slowing down for me. So as I mash on the accelerator, I look in that rearview mirror one more time…there you are….I say, **Fuck you Failure!**

This Stage #SpokenTruth
September 8, 2015

THIS STAGE that has given me the floor, has seen many wondrous performers such as I – this I know for sure...

From that nervous comedian that talks about his life and only wants to bring a smile to someone else's life even though his life is full of grief and strife; all he needs is your applause (clap, clap, clap,) and laughter (hahahaha) to help him ease his night.

This stage is for that R&B, rap, blues, pop, Indi, rock, gospel, hip-hop artist and vocalist who hope their voice won't crack before they leave the mic and cause the audience to snap, just like your mama's back.

This stage can bring a crowd to tears and cheers, watching actors reinvent, fine-tune and create simple words that were put upon our plate, so we put on a show that is sure to please the ticket gate.

This stage will bend and creak under the dancers' limbs whose guts are in a knot, knowing this might be their only shot - so they give it all they've got.

This stage is for that awkward kid in school who might have been picked on a time or two, but once they learned prestidigitation, sleight of hand, a few magic tricks or two then everyone thought they were cool.

This stage is for those of us who have beauty in our minds that we transcribe and translate to the world in glass, portrait, art, and print just to get it out of our minds.

This stage is for those chosen few who need no mic, no lights or huge crowd to seduce; for our words are spoken to keep you in tune with the tragic and beautiful life we go through.

This stage is for that seasoned vet whose life was no longer the same the day they took the crowd and made them say their name, or that rookie who's tried everything else but this final test of themselves.

This stage is not just performance, inspiration, or notches in our belts - it is our very life blood and soul we give to you the audience... because you could be anyplace else.

SPOKEN
TRUTH
BERNARD
BLM
MY WORDS ONLY
CHOICE
NO GMO
LIFE
I CAN'T BREATHE
LOVE
DR GRAY

Chapter 6

> I saw the line and crossed it without ever looking back; now I see the shadows of souls that need me to have their backs. – J. Summers

...Wake Up

Silent Face In The Crowd #SpokenTruth
April, 2015

I am an activist! I stand proud with my sign…it's my pen, my button, my banner, my voice, and my belief that I stand behind!

You may find me on the street corner or marching with other great minds.

We have been called names, spat upon, tear-gassed, hosed, and attacked by dogs 'sicced' on us…beaten, maimed, murdered and blamed. All because we believe it's our civil duty to speak out against great injustice and point out the ones that should feel ashamed! Ashamed of the silent murders they commit - poisoning our pipes with lead and filth, destroying the environment, and feeding us food that never had life in it. Crimes against humanity that make us sick, bombing women and children, clear/cutting forests, and killing kids over a bag of skittles and sip. All of this so they can become filthy rich!

Why do we care? You may ask as you sit behind your gates counting those blood-money stacks gained from great pain, while you build yourself up on the backs of corporate names! Because we may be the only ones who see through all the hateful lies and deceitful games you play with our peoples hopes and dreams. So we protest, demonstrate, organize, petition, educate, and *hell yes fight back*! Not for ourselves, but for our children, the planet, and those that have our back!

Because we want a world with more peace, more freedom of speech, not one filled with fear, hate, lies, discrimination, manipulation, or deceit!

And while you may silence one of us, there are millions more that have heard our desire, seen our fire, who now burn for something more! More than the spoon-fed media truth that you give to them, that you spin to them to corrupt their children and to no longer defend them!

I am an activist! I stand proud in my resolve; those that came before me strengthen me when I think I might fall…Sojourner Truth, Mahatma Gandhi, Nelson Mandela, Rosa Parks, Frederick Douglass, Marcus Garvey, Fred Hampton, Stokely Carmichael, Angela Davis, Malcolm X, and Martin Luther King, Jr.!

They knew they might fall. But what they did, they did for each and every last one of y'all.

Dear Mr. Trump
JANUARY 30, 2017

Dear Mr. Trump,

You will not run me out of my country, no matter how many walls, no matter how many ill-laws, or how much hate you try to spread.

I will not recognize you as my Leader because you do not give a fuck about the people! My ancestors, brothers and sisters bled, cried, screamed, and broke chains for their freedom.

Your pen will never be mightier than the people! The ink is all dried up, watered down with the tears of investment bankers and brokerage loans. The parchment you choose to write your broken bills on will never be accepted in my home! It's not even good for firewood, because it's been treated with prison loans, pipeline disasters waiting to happen, budget cuts for the rich, medical nightmares for the poor, and immigrants afraid to leave their homes!

Dear Mr. Trump,

The people are not a commodity for you to do with as you see fit. You cannot file us into bankruptcy or offshore accounts! We are not numbers to crunch or lawsuits to evade and we are not your bottom line! We are people, human beings, souls!

We are the life force of this country and if you push us, there will be no secret service, no wall can you build, no constitution or mandate you can create, nor any sign can you make that will keep us from finding you -- leaving behind nothing but spray tan imprints, scattered strands of hair, and a few hateful inaccurate Twitter lines.

So, Mr. Trump, straighten up! Please stand in line...

The whole country is watching you. We know where you live, the bunkers where you may try and hide; even Air Force One can't fly that high or keep you in the sky, when the country decides it's time to say goodbye.

Much love,

Sleep tight POTUS

The Last Day of Denise Clark
January 25, 2017

<u>The Last Day of Denise Clark</u>

A young woman died today. She lived on the fifth floor of the Bernard Building, Apartment C3. It was the most adequate place she could afford on her minimum wage job.

The Bernard Building sits on the edge of town in an urban sprawl. The building is dressed with chipping paint, and houses multiple bothersome squeaky floors. The security gate is broken unless you're trying to leave…then you need a key. The hallways are laced with junkies and the water has been contaminated for the past two years now. The central air works, but it blows heat in the summer and cold in the winter.

Denise Clark is late for work again because she cannot bathe, wash, or cook with water within a 3-mile radius of her apartment. The contaminated water sent her to the Urgent Care three times in the last two months. On her last visit, the doctors told her they could not do anything about the rash she developed on her neck. This visit, Dr. Enrique has papers on where she could get help for her addiction (for the third time). He patched up the marks on her arm as best as he could and sent her on her way, a procedure that caused her to be 45-minutes late for work.

Ken Stebenfield, her boss, understood Denise's situation and tried to be sympathetic. But he is burdened with his own bothersome issues - the upcoming election, his mortgage is due, his undocumented workers are about to go over the wall literally. When Denise comes in, he motions her to the back office. Mr. Stebenfield begins to scold her, (while also looking at her legs and breasts…not once looking at her face) reminding her tardiness must end and that this was her 'last chance'. He told Miss Clark he would deduct 3-hours from her pay or take her off the schedule for the weekend. He mentioned (as he motions over to the company calendar) he's off the weekend... and would forget about the whole situation if... she did him a *favor*.

Before she could respond, she noticed a most uncomfortable look on Mr. Stebenfield's face. Miss Clark had been scratching her arm the whole time and hadn't noticed the Band-Aid fell off and that blood was dripping down her arm from her most recent inoculation to get through the day. His face instantly turned red and he started yelling, cursing, and even threw something at the door. She left the office, and by the time she got to the front door he had come out of the office yelling, "You stupid, low income, drug addict, thot... you're fired!!!"

After 3 hours and 3 busses later (she missed the first bus trying to plead with Ken for her job), she explained to him the reasons she needed this job - she has no health care; this job was the only thing keeping her rent paid; her forced multiple trips to the ER from water poisoning; she had no food in the fridge, and was just hoping to just make it until tomorrow). Still he pointed her to the door.

(Continued)

(Continued)

Denise Clark climbs the five flights of stairs to her apartment. The elevator never worked and had been plastered over with club promotions from 4 years of failed attempts at trying to be a ballerina.

She sits on her couch and turns on the 9 year old TV; she starts flipping through channels but sees nothing other than the Trump inauguration.

Denise Clark's rent is three times the amount she has in her pocket.   She thinks to herself. Her arm begins to ache, her mind begins to race. She has finally had enough. Miss Clark goes over to the sink fills up two cups with water. She set the cups on the make-shift crate table in front the TV. She opens the apartment door and goes down the five flights of stairs and gives Jim two-thirds of what she has in her pocket (*why die broke?* she thinks), and then climbs back up the five flights of steps and prepares her getaway. As she walks back into her apartment, a strange sense of calm overtakes her as she listens to Trump's voice on the TV in the background.

She walks to the crate table where she left the cups and begins to drink. As she drinks the first glass with its coppery, bitter taste, she thinks about the protest she was involved in over the summer, the people she met, the friends she will never see again, and how she *wanted* to be better. Now, her getaway is beginning to take full effect and she can feel the tingling in her fingertips and toes. She takes the second glass, knowing she doesn't have much time, and screams, "Fuck You Trump! Drink up!"…as she hurls the second glass at the TV. The last thing she saw was the screen exploding.

Two weeks later, the door to the 5th floor Apartment C3 is kicked in. The door was barricaded with the empty refrigerator that had tattered note paper taped to the door that read, "*Fuck You Trump!! You can't grab this pussy*"!

The lifeless body of Miss Clark and the scorched floor around the TV was the only thing you could smell in the building for three months until, they too, became a distant memory.

The medical examiner's report read:

Name: Denise Clark
Sex: F
Age: 23
Cause of death: Overdose/lead poisoning
Next of kin: None
Case closed.

A young woman died today - no one shed a tear that she overdosed out of fear.

What Is C.O.T.S.? - Where the Ideal Began
January 2, 2015

For those who don't know me yet, I write how I talk; if you've met me in person you will see it rather quickly. I am C.O.T.S. - Child Of The System.

Why have I chosen this title? We are all children until we move on to the next life, whatever that may be. I chose this title for myself years ago because I've done so many different things in my one lifetime. But it's all been through one system or another. I have been a part of so many different things, walked so many different paths – some legal, some not. No matter what I've done, I understand that people become trapped in one system or another so they put up blinders to the rest of life. Rather it's the job they work, the religion they believe in, or the lifestyle they live they eventually become intricately trapped in that system – we all live on the same little blue sphere (maybe) speeding through millions of miles of cosmic soup. I don't know anyone, no matter where they are in life, who can say they're not part of that system.

When I speak to you under the title I use, the words I use come from *me*. I don't speak from motivations of promotion or entertainment, and I don't speak off the top of my head, but rather I speak from within as a result of everything I've done and have seen. Admit it or not, we're all trapped in a system.

SPOKEN
TRUTH
MY
WORDS
ONLY

Chapter 7

I am the most important person when I walk into a room only because of the experiences in my life that have led me to you. You are the most important person in the room because of the experiences that only you have lived through. – J. Summers

...Aftermath

Mist

April 2, 2017

Can you feel that vibration resonating in the air? Spine tingling, soul quenching, inspiration through thrust.

Fingers penetrating blank pages, leaving blood stained writings from your life's ink.

Ears scream and cream when you spit those things that hide in the dark places, under doubt, fake smiles, earth shattering truth and joy only you and your creator know.

Eyes awaking, seeing each stroke of the fear that leaves your vessel as you create your very own hope to keep pushing on.

Leaving marks on endorphin enriched pupils that learn to touch your soul.

Water
April 3, 2017

Pushing back the tears of a forgotten life, as they stain the rivers of memories and flow into the dreams of something new.

Cascading on the rocks of truth, I see my destiny through all the hardships I've been through.

Free to flow wherever I go, only bound by the gravity that controls every soul.

New horizons on the forecast and a sea of life to meet. It's time to transcend everything I thought I couldn't be.

Blink
April 8, 2017

Writing this journey down with the speed of my mind, taking photos that become manipulated over time.

Through eyes that were not there, so they speculate the memories in between.

Making friends in between blinks of locations that I couldn't possibly dream.

Traversing borders with ink, videos, speech, and thoughts of better things.

Notification
April 9, 2017

I guess what I really do is advertising.

I just don't see it that way honestly because it's my life on display.

I don't think when I post; I try and invoke some form of support from you and your fellow folks.

I never really notice until I'm with a friend, and their phone starts going off like they just won a lottery of friends.

They look over at me and say please stop posting... I smile and say thank you for noticing.

A King's Cypher
<u>April 10, 2017</u>

I was not raised by royalty, nor given servants to bow before me.

I have no land to survey or people that must obey every word that comes out of my mouth.

I only have the blood in my veins, the breath in my lungs, the idea that I want to see better for everyone, and the bruised memories of how much my people have suffered under thumb.

I am royalty without a crown. My skin glows with no jewels around; it is tinted by the kiss of the sun and the moon's tempering gaze, strengthened by the pain all my ancestors faced, and forged and fused out of the Creator's grace.

Protecting and preserving the future is my ultimate goal.

I will battle all enemies that wish harm to the family's stronghold. I am from the place leaders are built and trained to become kings and queens. A place that gave birth to great minds, scholars, protectors, and of those who would venture off to find truth by any means.

My crown should never shift or sway towards things that will hinder my people's dreams or keep them blind to corruptive ways.

I take no days off; I stand strong with a listening heart and lead when there is need for my people to succeed.

That is what it means to be a king for me.

All This Stuff
April 18, 2017

I have all this stuff now...things from places I've been, memories given to me by friends, boxes of awards and newspaper clippings and a closet of things my mind keeps forgetting.

I have all this stuff now...books that I've written, plays that I've been in, shows that I've hosted, organizations that I founded, dreams that I've given...and it just keeps building.

I do all this stuff now...I buy albums, art, books, venues, supplies, keepsakes, and try to provide.

There is nowhere I won't go...venues across the country, around the globe. Concerts, art shows, marches, protests, food shows, carnivals, clubs, community centers, churches and projects right outside your door.

I have a business to run and make sure it keeps its soul... I do not sell myself but I carry the message that everyone should achieve their goals.

My creation will outlive the Creator, if I only live my life...I will have something to leave the generations that could use some truth in their life.

Tempted
April 21, 2017

I want to wake up next to you...I want to feel the vibrations as we fold into each other's consciousness, warming sore muscles, kissing secret spots, and talking about our day.

I need to feel your comforting touch...gently caressing and dissolving away the stress of the day, wiping away the mistakes that I've made, bonding in sync as we apply pressure just the right way.

I am listening for your voice...waiting for your hypnotic, resonating gift to pierce my eardrums with the most undeniable truth I have ever heard.

Waiting, anticipation, dreaming...to witness the vision that is you. The one that will hold the throne next to me, adjust my crown when the weight bares too much on me, and who enriches my life with compassion, honesty, and leadership.

The one who is ready to build on what we've already accomplished individually, and is ready to take the next step.

Freewriting
April 23, 2017

Grasping at the paper as my life bleeds through the lines.

Writing my true-life story out, one verse at a time.

I bleed with the truth, as it runs through my veins. Unleashing cerebral synapses to burst with consciousness as my pen whips the page.

If only I could explain how to bottle, condense, rewrite, release, control, and articulate my emotions as I build through the pain.

Leaving nothing but glimpses of a life for individuals to translate.

Broken, emotional sentences flood through my mind granting my pen a beautiful cornucopia of limitless imagination... as simple words stream through soon to be opened eyes.

Gifted you might say, but nightmares I'll take to my grave with the words I didn't say. Lifetimes that got scribbled away and unanswered questions and memories I should have saved.

My words inspire me first, before any other human being. While I would love for you to listen, sit down, and read my dreams, they have to speak truth to me before anyone else - because this might be the only message that saves someone else.

Mic Check

April 24, 2017

Gliding on the vibrations of the audience, as I approach the mic...spitting fire, knowledge, truth, and respect as I invoke my words to take life.

God speech and forgotten dialect is what I bring tonight. No random verse or misused words that lead my people away from the truth and into trap star strife.

Speaking life to a soul that has never been told they matter or that their value is undeniable - you are creation.

As we sync through these 26 divine letters of inspiration, the world begins to unfold; all the secrets of the mortal coil are left for you to expose. Tortured by a past which most artists lie to create. Cycling through lifetimes I can only hope to change for better days.

Art is my life, ink is my blood, tendons, muscles, and cartilage; my bones are strengthened by the fans that keep me whole...encased in the epidermis of faith. Through my grind, I'll never grow old.

15 Min
April 28, 2017

22 birthdays, 15 missed messages, 3,000 comments, 1,000 replies, 45,000 views, 1 missed call, and 35 new likes... is what I see when I unlock my screen.

22 birthdays, 15 missed messages, 3,000 comments, 1,000 replies, 45,000 views, 1 missed call, and 35 new likes... is the price I pay for the opportunity to change the world I see today.

22 birthdays, 15 missed messages, 3,000 comments, 1,000 replies, 45,000 views, 1 missed call, and 35 new likes... that keep growing everyday as I push through the pain.

22 birthdays, 15 missed messages, 3,000 comments, 1,000 replies, 45,000 views, 1 missed call, and 35 new likes... souls I may never meet, but I am empowered by the support they offer my way. Never knowing what it took to grace the stage, hold a sign, speak my truth, and stand in defiance of every injustice that every human grows through.

22 birthdays, 15 missed messages, 3,000 comments, 1,000 replies, 45,000 views, 1 missed call, and 35 new likes... adjusted through the kaleidoscope of social media and bonding moments just for the idea to grow; you are never alone as long as you stay true to your individual soul.

11 birthdays, 5 missed messages, 1,000 comments, 350 replies, 22 new photos... most of the day is done and I will never know the full impact of what I've said online, but it's time I move my feet. Time to pound the pavement and get away from this screen. I can't change the world just writing, when my experiences give my pen ink.

200 comments, 22 missed messages, 2,000 replies, 1 new photo... Goodnight. Thank you Creator for guiding my light.

Round 2
April 29, 2017

Loading up my verbal chamber with nine clips, but I'll only need 3 to finish off the round. Buck shots so to clear to the crowd, hollow points to zero in and armor-piercing for the last round.

A lethal injection concocted through the wordplay of my life, but the only bodies that will hit the floor will be conscious minds as I spit my truth tonight.

No need to shy away, I am only vibrating with the life that I built through the pain... resonating with memories of long forgotten friends shattered by the crippling voice that creeps in every crack and crevice your soul tries to reseal again.

Laying these chains in the dirt to collect rust and be broken... no slave tunes here, this is pure emotion.

Lines of devastation that bleed through my rhythm, leaving stroke symptoms as I purge this venom.

Clear Eye's #SpokenTruth
April 30, 2017

I cried for you...
Every time I try to push away the pain, I am reminded - I cried for you.

I cried for you...
Because of you I was foolish enough to fall to for the empty promises of how there would be no more scars on my heart, no more days where I would just sit up and look at the blank wall searching for answers as the tears run down my swollen face.

I cried for me...
I told my heart not to worry! I told my heart that enough time had passed - that the scar tissue, stitches, bruised left ventricle, and overworked carotid arteries would finally be receiving better days. I convinced my blood not to run cold - that there would be one soul that would emerge and mend this duct-taped, government-funded disaster, and pay the tolls that life racked up that wasn't always my fault.

I cried for truth...
Because of you, every face that I see becomes a smile; a crooked little grin that screams *I know the reason you're here! I know every little secret you're trying to hide behind your eyes. I know every failure, every mistake, every microscopic meticulous reason you deserved to fail! And no matter how many streams, rivers, lakes or oceans of tears fall from your face, I will ask for more because you haven't shown me enough!*

I cried for death...
But the tears never came. The salty secretions that drenched my face and engraved tombstones of irritated/battered pores, and that consoled my pillows with an oasis of floodwaters have finally stopped today.

I wiped away my last tear today...
I stood to my feet, ground up every ounce of doubt within me and walked calmly towards my destiny. The last tear to fall took with it the best memory all.

You *should* have cried the day you forgot about me.

Something Happy
MAY 1, 2017

Someone once told me to write something happy; write something for the kids. Talk about your childhood and all the friends you played with.

Someone once told me to write something happy; leave behind something that doesn't make us cry, doesn't send us down a mental mind-blowing experience where your pain becomes our life, your distant memories become a transfixed template, engraved in our minds image of you.

Someone once told me to write something happy; something that even though they love what I write, must I always try to bring some truth to light? Can't I write a verse about pools of lipid filled gas elements of pure beauty?
Don't I see happiness?

Someone once told me to write something happy, I quickly reply, "I am happy! You see what you want to see, but I am writing my dreams…living life and letting my pen guide my light through a legacy of people who need a friend that understands them and the pain they'll never speak. I'm taking a chance while I still have my mind to transition between my life and the life of my pen."

Someone once told me to write something happy...
I told them, "Let me grab my pen."

<u>N</u>ostalgic <u>I</u>nformation <u>G</u>lamorizing <u>G</u>raveyard <u>A</u>dventures
#SpokenTruth
MAY 25, 2017

Gun clicks... Pow!

Don't be so alarmed...it's just the sound of another Nigga dead! Another brown boy lay dead in the streets by the hands of someone who does not wear a badge. A boy whose skin is melaninated to just the right tint, where this is no longer a crime!
This story will never see the news, except to dig up old wounds and remind you all the reasons he deserved to die!

It's just gang violence…the results of a life they chose to live. It's not a reflection on our community. There are no invisible walls connected to the gold chain trap music and influence that we feed you while we rape your mind, steal your childhood, erase your history, and convince you that living on assistance is the quickest way to get out. One platinum, drug-tested epidemic streams through our children's eyes; one flat line at a time.

I thought you should know his name was Tyrone; he leaves behind three kids at home – he died without a dime.

Gun clicks... Pow!

No need to grab your signs, protest in the streets, or write your congressman a hateful letter...it's just another nigga dead! Another young woman lost to the streets who was molested as a child by pastors, teaches, parents, and trusted family members. So, she left home trying to find a way to survive and although she was young, she had already gone numb, deciding this is how she would survive. She did pretty well and manage to scrape by until someone viewed her as a prize. A money-making scheme to get rich quick is how he came. But when she decided it was time to get ghost, they ditched her quick.

(Continued)

(Continued)

One shot to the gut and a twist of the neck…left in a dumpster for 3 weeks to set. Her family had no clue; they were all too busy trying to hide the shame they felt, the fear they had of the truth coming out; still they all knew. So, her case sits in a stack of unsolved murders - Jane Doe, with the description torn out.

Bars clink... Pow!

Unless you go to where lost children become lost souls, you will never know how deep the extermination goes - but it's just another nigga dead!

The last sound they'll hear before joining a company of their peers who were told in school they were never good enough; they were too hyperactive; their grades were no good; they might have played sports but their teachers read from books. They had no sense of structure - just fall in line... your creativity can only fit on the dotted line.

So the system passed them by, determined that by the third grade their resting place, if the curriculum doesn't fit their age, is concrete walls. Now, it's prison guards - just three strikes away, or one if you multiply just the right way a shiny new workforce at just 10 cents a day! Soon they'll be released back to the streets with a criminal record and no way out; but the streets will pay the way...the bars become their church bells they'll ring to their grave.

But don't shed a tear because these statistics were just born out of fear. It's time to come out of the dark and speak light to your loved ones while they still have ears that hear the right way.

Fin...

LIFE
TEARS
OF
DEATH
THE WOUNDID
NOL2